JOURNEY TO THE RESURRECTION

Rose Visual Bible Studies

ROSE PUBLISHING

Journey to the Resurrection
Rose Visual Bible Studies

Published by Rose Publishing
An imprint of Tyndale House Ministries
Carol Stream, Illinois
www.hendricksonrose.com

ISBN 978-1-62862-808-1

Author: Titus O'Bryant, ThM, Teaching Pastor, Grace Fellowship Church

Book design by Cristalle Kishi.

Printed in the United States of America
030124VP

Contents

"Praise be to the God and
Father of our Lord Jesus Christ!

In his great mercy he has given
us new birth into a living hope
through the resurrection of
Jesus Christ from the dead."

1 Peter 1:3

Journey to the Resurrection

Travel can be tiring, but also very rewarding. When I first started taking road trips, I used a road atlas to plan my journeys. Today, I use an app on my phone. My traveling companions and I take time to consider where we might stop along the way to stretch our legs and how we'll pass the time on the road. With any road trip, the final destination gives shape to the rest of the journey.

You and I are embarking on a well-traveled road. We are following along the path that Jesus walked as he moved toward his death and ultimately his resurrection. This is a journey like no other. Along the way, we'll stop at a few critical junctions in the life of Jesus before we gaze at the cross and, finally, the empty tomb.

Junction #1: At his baptism, Jesus starts his public ministry with his final destination clearly in view. He identifies himself with the sins of all people and foreshadows the way he will lay down his life in sacrifice and take it up again in resurrection.

Junction #2: Jesus enters the wilderness for forty days, where he fasts and is challenged by the tempter. In the forty days leading to Easter, we mimic Jesus' forty days of testing by engaging in spiritual practices that prepare our hearts for his resurrection.

Junction #3: Here we pivot toward the final week of Jesus' ministry before his death. A woman prepares Jesus for his burial with an act of devotion and generosity that Jesus holds up as a model for all who would follow him.

Junction #4: We join Jesus and his disciples at the Passover table for a final meal. Jesus expresses the depth of his power in an amazing act of humble service as he washes each of his disciples' feet to instruct us about what it looks like to serve others.

Finally, we arrive at the cross of Jesus. We remember that what appears to be defeat is actually the victory of God over evil.

But this journey doesn't end at the cross on Good Friday. The cross leads to resurrection life. We join in the wonder and awe of those followers of Jesus who peered into the empty tomb that Sunday morning. In celebrating the resurrection, we find hope that can fill every moment of our lives.

In the early church, the forty-six days (forty if you subtract the Sundays) prior to Easter presented an opportunity for new believers to prepare for uniting with the church by baptism. This time period came to be known as Lent. Early believers were leaving behind old religions and customs, and they intentionally took time to investigate the claims of Jesus and examine their own soul before finally committing to Christianity.

Today, for some Christians, Lent represents a shared spiritual practice rich with meaning. Other believers may be alarmed by the idea of Lent, considering it a stale tradition or even a harmful form of legalism. Regardless of our different church traditions or backgrounds, all Christians can claim the season before Easter as an opportunity to become more aware of the weakness within us and our world and to chase after Jesus instead of the lesser pursuits that often claim our attention.

1 DUST AND ASHES

Confession

Dust and Ashes

Ashes to ashes and dust to dust . . . in the sure and certain hope of the resurrection of the dead.

You have probably heard these words spoken at a funeral or burial service. As a pastor, I've spoken them many times. They are words intended to benefit the living, not the dead. We remember that our lifetime will come to an end, but also that hope for the life to come can shape and provide direction for the way we live right now. When we begin with the end in mind, all of our actions, decisions, and attitudes help us intentionally make progress toward our anticipated final destination.

Jesus began his public ministry with a clear-eyed vision directed toward his final destination. He knew exactly how the story of his public life and ministry would end, but he also believed that the end of his story would be the beginning of new life for him and for all who trust in him. His public ministry, which would lead to a cross and an empty tomb, began with his baptism.

Read It

Key Bible Passage

For this session, read the story of Jesus' baptism in Matthew 3:1–17.

Optional Reading

See how the apostle Paul connects our baptism with Christ's death and resurrection in Romans 6:1–11.

"Confessing their sins, they were baptized by [John] in the Jordan River."

MATTHEW 3:6

Know It

1. What was John the Baptist's primary message and how did the crowds respond?

2. Jesus said he wanted to be baptized in order to "fulfill all righteousness" (Matthew 3:15). How did he accomplish this in his baptism?

3. How does John the Baptist describe Jesus to the crowds? How does God the Father (the voice from heaven) describe him?

Explore It

Baptism

John the Baptist's practice of baptism grew out of the Jewish tradition of ritual washing. We can learn more about the significance of baptism by exploring these ancient practices.

To baptize (*baptizō* in Greek) means to dip or immerse and refers to ritual and spiritual cleansing that comes from an act of washing in water. In the Old Testament, baptism or ritual washing was used by priests for sacrifices and to maintain ritual purity.

- New priests were washed when beginning their office (Exodus 29:21; Leviticus 8:6).
- Priests washed their hands before completing sacrifices (Exodus 30:17–21).
- The high priest washed himself before and after sacrifices on the Day of Atonement (Leviticus 16:1–28).
- Ritually unclean people and objects were washed (Leviticus 11:24–40; 12–15).

Medieval Mikvah (Jewish ritual bath)

Both before and after the time of Jesus, various types of baptism were practiced.

- The Qumran community was a separatist, Jewish sect living near the Dead Sea around 100 BC. They believed that they were the only surviving remnant faithful to God's covenant and practiced daily baptism or ceremonial cleansing as part of their covenant community.

- Judaism permitted gentiles to convert by following certain guidelines: studying the Hebrew Scriptures, becoming circumcised (for males), and completing several ritual obligations that culminated in a ritual bath (baptism) to leave impurities behind and be reborn into the Jewish faith. Baptism for gentile converts likely began near the end of the first century AD.

John's baptism was available to all "who repent of their sins and turn to God" (Matthew 3:11 NLT). Crowds visited John in the wilderness by the Jordan River to confess their sins and "wash away" the impurities in their lives. They would rise up out of the water and symbolically leave their sin, shame, and guilt behind.

Jordan River

Jesus had no sins to repent of or turn away from, yet he insisted on being baptized. Part of the significance of Jesus' baptism is that all of the sins left behind by people (in fact, all humanity) were received by and placed on Jesus.

Baptism also represented death (being laid down in the water) and resurrection (being raised out of the water). Jesus' ultimate aim—becoming our sin substitute and making new life possible for all who believe—is foreshadowed in his baptism at the very beginning of his public ministry.

Live It

Jesus doesn't condemn us. He came into our world to offer us forgiveness and new life. No action, spiritual practice, or work that we perform earns God's blessing or forgiveness. We receive Jesus' righteousness as a free gift when we trust in him and his completed work for us—when we place our confidence in his life, death, and resurrection as the means that bridges the gap between us and the life God offers.

As we follow Jesus, confessing and turning away from our sins and failures becomes an important spiritual practice. God uses this to help us keep growing as he shapes our character to become more like Jesus. God provides the power that changes us. We can be obedient to his call to live devoted to him and in the reality of his forgiveness.

Life Application Questions

1. Why is confessing our sin—out loud, in writing, in prayer, or directly to another person—so difficult?

2. Can you remember a significant moment when you confessed sin or failure to another person—or when someone confessed to you? What was that experience like and how did it affect you and your relationship with the other person?

3. How would you describe what it means that Jesus took our sin upon himself or became sin for us? (Read 2 Corinthians 5:21 and 1 Peter 3:18 for additional context.)

4. Are there any ways that you hold on to the sins that Jesus carried away from you? What makes it challenging to release these sins?

5. How would your life be different if you were to live each and every day in the enduring truth and reality of the freedom that comes from forgiveness?

6. We have been freely forgiven by Jesus. Is there anyone in your life (living or dead) whom you need to forgive, whether they have asked for forgiveness or not? If so, what has been holding you back from forgiving them?

Spiritual Discipline: Confession

Practicing spiritual disciplines in the weeks leading to the celebration of Jesus' death and resurrection can prepare our hearts to fully embrace the significance of those moments.

We often think of confessing our sins only as part of the beginning of our relationship with Jesus, where we acknowledge our failure and turn to faith in the finished work of Jesus. Confession does not end with our conversion, but continues throughout our life to keep leading us to the freedom we enjoy in Jesus. Confession involves your entire being: mind, heart, and soul. It includes thoroughly examining yourself, feeling the emotional response of sorrow because of sin, and then determining to turn away from those sins with the power of the Holy Spirit.

Ash Wednesday

Many Christians begin Lent by observing Ash Wednesday. This is a day to intentionally turn away from our failings and lesser pursuits that sometimes cause us to miss the best that God has planned for us.

The palms used to celebrate Palm Sunday from the previous year are burned, and the ashes kept. On Ash Wednesday, they are used to place the sign of the cross on the foreheads of worshipers. This is a reminder that our life here is temporary. We are made of dust and will return to dust, but through Jesus we also receive the blessing of life beyond this life.

Here is a guide for confession for you to consider:

1. Write down the sins you are guilty of: pride, greed, anger, fear, laziness, gluttony, lust, hate, etc.
2. Confess (speak out loud) these sins to God.
3. Remember the promise: "If we confess our sins to him, he is faithful and just to forgive us our sins and to cleanse us from all wickedness" (1 John 1:9 NLT).
4. Tear that paper into as many pieces as possible and throw it away, or, if you prefer, burn it.
5. If you have a trusted friend, you can confess your sins to that person and involve them in this process. There is something liberating about bringing our sins out from the dark and into the light, and feeling God set us free.

Prayer

Lord Jesus, thank you for taking all of my sin on yourself, becoming sin for me, and giving your life so I can enjoy new life. Give me the grace to live in this new freedom and in victory over the power of sin. Amen.

Notes

Notes

2 IN THE WILDERNESS

Fasting

In the Wilderness

Just after Jesus was baptized to begin his public ministry, he experienced a private testing and temptation. Led by the Holy Spirit, he walked into the wilderness alone, stayed there for forty days and nights, fasted from eating food, and was challenged by the tempter, who tried to deceive, discourage, and defeat him. Jesus resisted the devil's attacks and rested in the truth of God's promise and in the security of his relationship with his Father.

The forty-day time period is significant and intentional. Jesus was following the example of Moses, who spent forty days on Mount Sinai receiving the old covenant from God (Exodus 24:18).

Jesus' forty days of testing also provides an example for us of facing and overcoming temptation. Like Jesus, we enter wilderness periods of life. Sometimes these seasons catch us by surprise. At other times, we know they are coming, but there is nothing we can do to avoid them. We may experience private times of trial and suffering, strong temptations and the results of our failure, or the challenges that come with the passing of time and stages of life. These seasons remind us of our weakness and limitations and our need to depend on the power and grace of our Savior.

Read It

Key Bible Passage

For this session, read the story of Jesus in the wilderness in Matthew 4:1–11.

Optional Reading

Read the story of the first temptation at the beginning of creation in Genesis 3:1–24.

"Jesus answered, 'It is written: Man shall not live on bread alone, but on every word that comes from the mouth of God.'"

MATTHEW 4:4

Know It

1. Jesus' wilderness time wasn't an accident. He intentionally confronted hunger and the devil. Why do you think Jesus chose to do this just after his baptism and before he began to preach publicly?

2. What motivation does the tempter appeal to in each of the three temptations?

#1. (verse 3): ______________________________

____

#2. (verses 5–6): ______________________________

____

#3. (verses 8–9): ______________________________

____

3. How does Jesus respond to each temptation?

#1. (verse 4): ______________________________

____

#2. (verse 7): ______________________________

____

#3. (verse 10): ______________________________

____

What stands out to you or surprises you? What is similar or different about each response?

Explore It

Temptation is not in itself sinful, and it does not necessarily result in sinful actions. The New Testament Greek word most often used to describe temptation is *peirasmos*. This word can refer to temptation toward sin or evil, but it can also refer to a testing or time of trial. It's used in ancient Greek literature to describe the process of refining gold, where gold is mined from rock and then undergoes *peirasmos*. This testing or refining brings the precious metal out of the rock and also demonstrates that it really is gold.

Refining gold

We know that God does not tempt us with evil. He does not pull us toward sin. James writes about both testing and temptation and reminds us that we can never claim that God is tempting us:

> Blessed is the one who perseveres under trial because, having stood the test, that person will receive the crown of life that the Lord has promised to those who love him. (James 1:12–13)

However, life does bring us to times of testing; seasons that put our character and our faith to the test; times when we're thrown into the fire. It is in those moments of life that the tempter comes to try to ruin our character and steal away our trust and confidence in God our Father. It is in those moments that evil is present, waiting to snatch us up.

Darrell Johnson, writing about this dynamic, observed, "There are events or experiences in life through which the Father intends to prove and improve our character and faith, but the evil one sneaks in and intends to destroy our character and faith."

Times of trial—when we feel intense pressure or face unexpected circumstances—normally include temptations toward evil: harmful attitudes, wrong actions, unhealthy thoughts, uncaring words. We are at a weak point when we are under stress. Our enemy knows this and tries to take advantage. When we face times of testing, we do not want or need to fall toward evil. This is why Jesus taught us to pray:

> Our Father who is in heaven,
> Hallowed be Your name.
> Your kingdom come.
> Your will be done,
> On earth as it is in heaven.
>
> Give us this day our daily bread.
> And forgive us our debts,
> as we also have forgiven our debtors.
> ***And do not lead us into temptation,***
> ***but deliver us from evil.***
>
> MATTHEW 6:9–13 NASB *(emphasis added)*

"Temptation is to the alienation of our souls. . . . Lord, when I have the inclination to sin, keep me from the opportunity; and when I have the opportunity, keep me from the inclination."

—HADDON ROBINSON

Live It

The tempter approaches us at our weakest point. He came to Jesus when Jesus was tired, hungry, and isolated. We should expect to face temptation when we are feeling weak. The strategies that our enemy employs are not new. He repeats the same patterns over and over because he has often found them to be successful.

Periods of temptation are an effort from the evil one to ruin our lives, reputation, and character. But they are also an opportunity for the Lord to step in and snatch away the victory that the devil thinks he has over us. God can use trials to improve our character and faith and demonstrate the quality of our relationship with him.

Fresco of Temptation of Jesus

Life Application Questions

1. How would you describe a "wilderness" experience in your past—or maybe one you're in now?

2. Can you recall a time when you gave in to temptation? What contributed to your failure? Can you recall a time when you successfully resisted temptation? Why were you successful?

3. Considering your weaknesses and strengths, where might you be vulnerable to a temptation pulling you toward evil?

4. Read 1 Corinthians 10:12–13 and 1 Peter 5:8–10. How do these Bible passages guide and encourage us to resist temptation?

5. Is there someone you know who is going through a wilderness season of life? How could you help them in this time?

6. When you face a testing that is likely to include temptation, plan in advance the best way to respond. What are three actions you could take or principles you could follow?

- ____

- ____

- ____

Spiritual Discipline: Fasting

When Jesus entered the wilderness, he stopped eating food. In the Bible, fasting means setting aside a period of time to abstain from food needed for our physical life in order to concentrate on our spiritual life. No biblical command dictates that Christians must fast in order to please God. However, Jesus fasted and indicated in Matthew 9:15 that his followers would also fast in the future.

Fasting is not practiced for health benefits, to manipulate God into giving us what we want, or to earn any blessing or special standing with God. Fasting helps us turn our attention away from ourselves and toward God. It helps us become more aware of our dependence on him.

Here are some suggestions to get you started:

1. Before beginning your fast (especially a long fast), consult with your doctor to discuss any potential health risks or ongoing health conditions. Your doctor can be a key component in helping you find a good strategy for fasting.

2. Start by fasting from one meal a day for one or more days. You could spend that mealtime instead in prayer and meditation on God's Word. You could also donate the money you'd normally spend on food to a worthy cause.

3. Next, fast for a twenty-four-hour period from lunchtime to lunchtime. Skip three meals (lunch, dinner, breakfast) spread over two days. Drink plenty of water and perhaps fruit juices during the fast.

4. Do this once a week for two or three weeks before attempting to fast for a longer period of time such as thirty-six to seventy-two hours.

5. Use your hunger as an opportunity to remember your weakness and express your dependence on God. Jesus himself said that we don't live on bread alone.

Prayer

Lord, I am weak, but you are strong. Give me the courage and wisdom to find your strength in my moments of weakness. Help me depend on the power that you provide instead of my own efforts. Thank you for giving me everything I need, including a way to escape my temptations. Amen.

Fasting

The *Didache* is an early instruction booklet for Christians from around AD 300. It provides insight into the habits of early Christians. Drawing a contrast with Jewish patterns of fasting, this book instructs Jesus-followers, "You should fast on Wednesday and Friday." For many early Christians, fasting was part of their regular, weekly routine of spiritual life.

Today, many Christians observe Lent, a forty-day period, as a reminder of Jesus' forty days in the wilderness. They fast from eating meat on Fridays during Lent and on special days like Ash Wednesday.

Notes

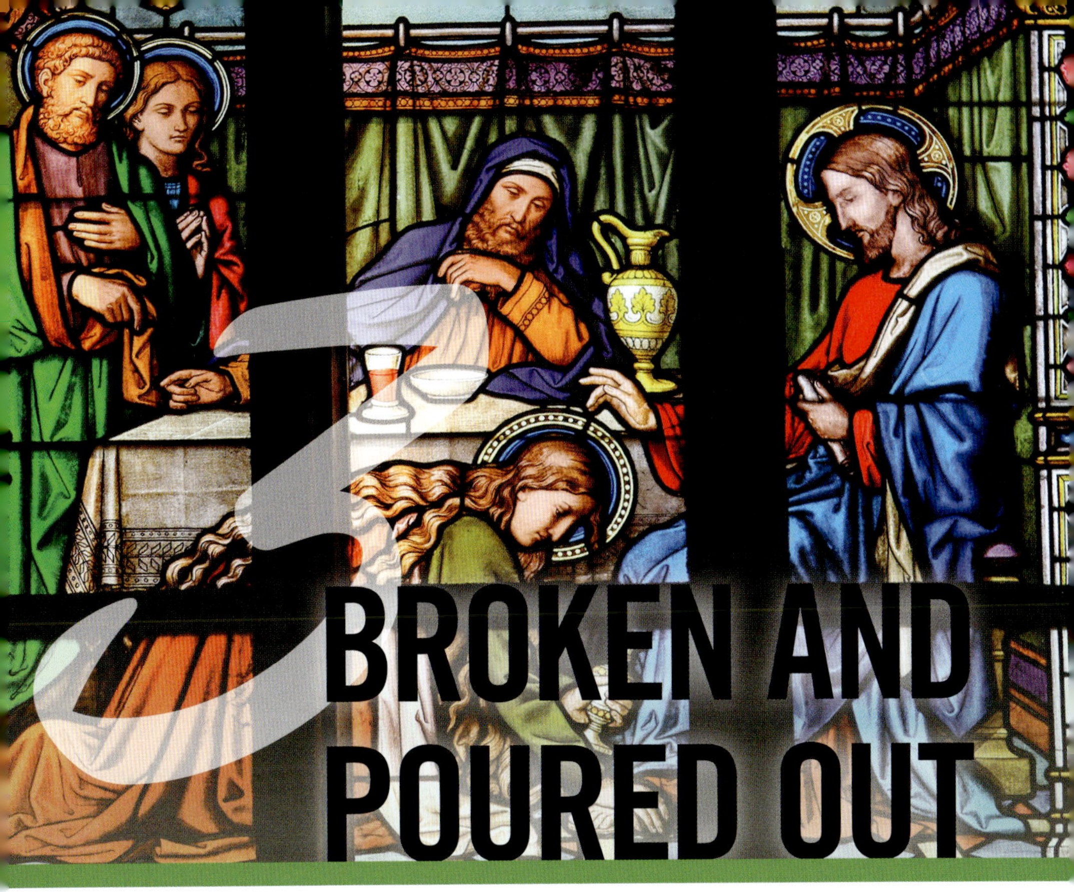

3 BROKEN AND POURED OUT

Generosity

Broken and Poured Out

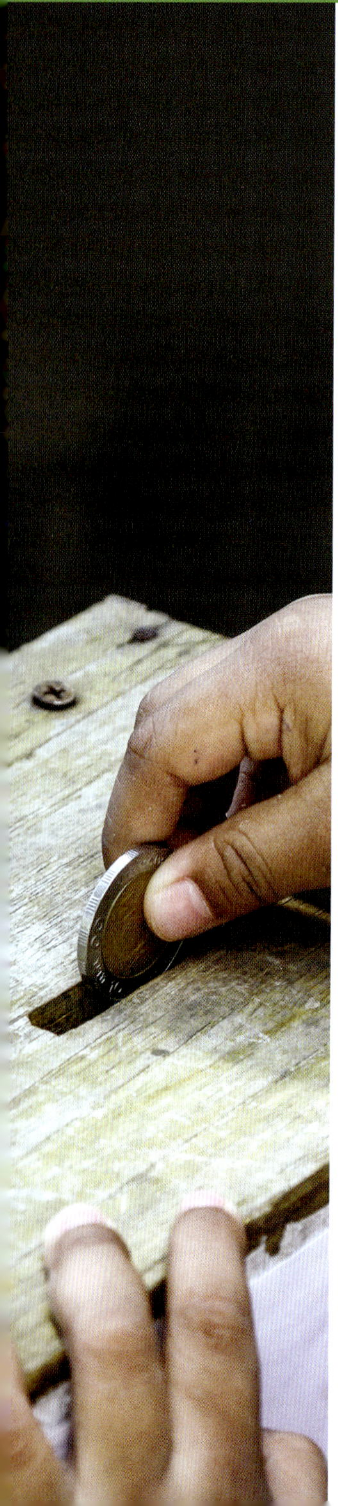

In the small town of Bethany, not far from Jerusalem, an unnamed woman approached Jesus just days before he would die. She anointed him with an expensive perfume as if he were a king or a Messiah, or similar to the way a body would be anointed at burial.

This woman demonstrated an understanding about Jesus, his mission, and what following him would mean that seemed to elude the other disciples. She taught them (and teaches us) what it means to follow the Lord.

Just like this woman's extravagant gift was broken and poured out, Jesus soon gave his own body to be broken and his blood to be poured out in death. He calls us to follow in the same path.

Read It

Key Bible Passage

For this session, read the story of Jesus being anointed in Mark 14:1–11.

Optional Reading

Read the parallel accounts of this story in Matthew 26:1–16 and John 12:1–11.

(Luke 7:36–50 also contains a similar story, but the setting, timing, and details are very different, and likely represent a different event.)

"She did what she could. She poured perfume on my body beforehand to prepare for my burial."

MARK 14:8

Know It

1. How many contrasts can you identify between the characters and their actions in this story? How does the woman compare to the disciples? To Judas?

2. Why might Mark have constructed this account to draw attention to these contrasts? (Compare it to the accounts in Matthew 26:1–16 and John 12:1–11.)

3. Imagine that you were present in the room when this extravagant gesture took place. How might you have felt and reacted? Would you have been among those who saw it as a waste of an expensive commodity?

Explore It

Do you have a favorite sandwich? Nothing else quite tastes like a nice Reuben, but my favorite type of sandwich is a "sandwich story." This is a technique that Mark uses several times throughout his gospel, where he "sandwiches" an inner story between two halves of an outer story to emphasize the point he is making. He starts by telling one story, then he moves on to another story entirely, before coming back to finish the original story he started with. This draws a sharp contrast between the characters, their actions and motivations, and the unique settings of the "bread" (outer story) and the "meat" (inner story).

SANDWICH STORY: MARK 14:1–11

Outer Story (verses 1–2): The religious leaders plot to arrest and kill Jesus.

Inner Story (verses 3–9): A woman anoints Jesus in preparation for burial.

Outer Story (verses 10–11): Judas and the religious leaders conspire to arrest Jesus.

This story in Mark 14 begins in the temple precincts where the powerful insiders of the establishment meet together to plot Jesus' arrest and death. The chief priests and rabbis would have been gathered in Jerusalem to celebrate the Feast of Unleavened Bread.

Then the scene switches to a group of outsiders in the small village of Bethany about one and a half miles from Jerusalem, in the home of a man identified as an outcast—Simon, who lived with the label "leper." (Perhaps he was one who had been healed by Jesus and now hosted Jesus and his followers.)

The Setting: During dinner, as the guests reclined on the floor with their heads near a low table and their feet further away, a woman enters the room. It wasn't unusual to anoint the head of a special guest or visiting rabbi with a couple drops of oil as a sign of welcome and honor.

The Sacrifice: But this woman carries a small stone container, probably holding about twelve ounces of purest perfume, oil made from the spikenard root growing far to the east in India. The container is alabaster, a soft stone that looks like marble. Instead of carefully releasing a few drops of this very expensive oil, she breaks off the narrow neck. The house is filled with the scent as she pours it on Jesus' head. John tells us that she also anoints Jesus' feet and wipes them with her hair. Some of the disciples become indignant, possibly because of what they would have seen as her forward behavior, but very directly about what they describe as an extravagant waste.

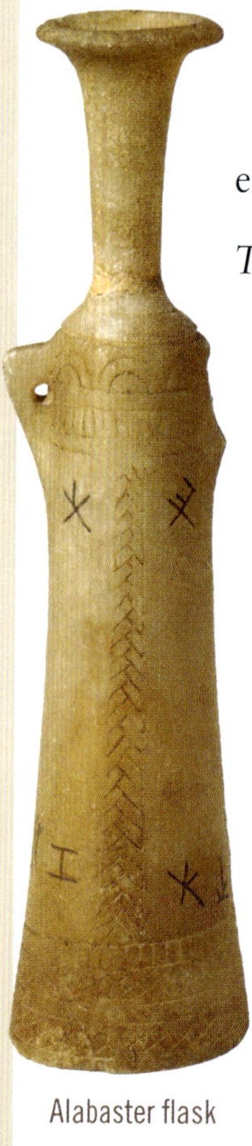
Alabaster flask

The Significance: This perfume may have represented her savings, her nest egg for the future, or maybe she had been keeping it for her own burial. Its value was estimated to be at least three hundred denarii or a year's working wage. (By the way, do you remember the amount that Judas received for betraying Jesus? Thirty shekels of silver or one hundred and twenty denarii.)

Jesus uses an intriguing phrase to describe this woman's sacrifice for him. In verse 8, Jesus says, "She did what she could." The Greek verbal root word that Mark uses for *could* comes from a verb meaning "to have" or "to hold." Mark uses a different form of this same verb just a page or so earlier in Mark 12 to describe another woman, the widow who came to the temple and offered pennies. Jesus noticed and praised her gift even while others gave far larger donations. Jesus said she had given more than all the rest because it was everything she *had* (that's our key verb).

She did what she could. (Mark 14:8)

She gave what she had. (Mark 12:44)

Both women gave extravagantly. Both of these Jesus-followers teach us that Jesus is looking for uncalculating devotion to himself, rather than supposedly fine wisdom and balanced judgment in giving.

Roman denarii

Never Forgotten

Mark was a careful storyteller, even mentioning details such as how the jar was made of alabaster and the perfume of pure nard. But, interestingly, he leaves out the name of the woman who anointed Jesus. (John's gospel identifies her as Mary, the sister of Lazarus and Martha.) Why this omission in Mark? Because it draws out an important contrast to express a deeper truth beneath the story. Mark omits the woman's name, but includes the name of Judas. This unnamed woman will never be forgotten because Jesus holds her up as an enduring beacon of faithful sacrifice, while Judas's name lives only in shame (Mark 14:9). She is a reminder that even if we feel overlooked, Jesus sees and knows us and the small and great sacrifices we make for him.

Live It

Throughout this section of Mark's gospel, Jesus had been telling his closest followers that he would soon die a horrible death (Mark 8:31–33; 9:31–34; 10:32–40). But they could never imagine a kingdom that would begin with the death of their friend and leader. Their idea of a kingdom required the death of their enemies, not their friend. They responded to his predictions by rebuking him for saying such things and by arguing about which one of them was the greatest—even asking Jesus to give them places of honor next to his throne.

The woman in this story in Mark 14 stands apart from the rest and is honored for her act of devotion. Jesus explained, "She poured perfume on my body beforehand to prepare for my burial. Truly I tell you, wherever the gospel is preached throughout the world, what she has done will also be told, in memory of her" (Mark 14:8–9).

After Jesus predicted his death in Mark 8, he called out to the crowds to join his followers. Listen to how he encouraged them to follow him:

> Whoever wants to be my disciple must deny themselves and take up their cross and follow me. For whoever wants to save their life will lose it, but whoever loses their life for me and for the gospel will save it. What good is it for someone to gain the whole world, yet forfeit their soul? Or what can anyone give in exchange for their soul? (Mark 8:34–37)

The call to us remains the same.

Life Application Questions

1. When have you experienced someone giving you an extravagant gift or act of kindness? How did that make you feel? How did you react?

2. How would you describe what it means to give extravagantly for the Lord? What does that look like? (Remember, "extravagant" doesn't necessarily mean "expensive." The poor widow gave only pennies.)

3. In the outer story, Jesus incited conflict with the leaders of Israel that would lead to his death (Mark 14:1–2, 10–11). This woman, in following Jesus, sparked a conflict among the disciples (Mark 14:4–5). (And imagine the inner conflict of the woman, who was harshly criticized by the disciples.) How have you experienced conflict because you follow Jesus? Did you have peace even when surrounded by conflict?

4. Read 2 Corinthians 2:14–16. In what ways can our lives be a pleasing aroma, lifting up to God?

5. Read Romans 12:1–2. What is God calling us to? Can you identify the inner and outer pressures a person committed to sacrificing themselves to the Lord might face?

6. What has God given you—time, a skill, an experience (perhaps one you really didn't want), resources, wisdom or perspective, influence, relationships, a family, a church, a workplace? How could you give back to him what he has trusted you with?

Spiritual Discipline: Generosity

We give ourselves and our resources back to God out of gratitude for what he has given us in Jesus. We are heirs to divine promises, children born into the family of God, set free from the harmful habits that once defined our lives. We now have the opportunity to share what we have received with others and to invest in the work that God is doing in our world. Here are a few principles from Paul's instructions to the church in Corinth that can guide our generous giving.

- **Give regularly:** "on the first day of every week" (1 Corinthians 16:2).
- **Give individually:** "each one of you should set aside" (1 Corinthians 16:2).
- **Give proportionately:** "in keeping with your income" (1 Corinthians 16:2).
- **Give willingly:** "not reluctantly or under compulsion" (2 Corinthians 9:7).
- **Give cheerfully:** "God loves a cheerful giver" (2 Corinthians 9:7).

You may discover a special project at your church that you could help fund, or perhaps it is time for you to reexamine the proportion of your income that you give away. Maybe you know someone or a group of people with a need in your community that you could help. Your Bible study group might consider pooling resources together to help support a mission project.

If you make yourself available to God, he will guide you in how he wants to use your resources.

Prayer

Lord, fill us with gratitude for your grace and love so that we respond by giving ourselves to you and to your work in our world. Grant us the courage to lay down our lives and do our very best to honor you. Thank you for the example of this woman, who loved you so much that she gave all she had. Help us to do the same. Amen.

Almsgiving

At certain times of the year—such as Christmas, Easter, or Thanksgiving—many churches will often provide special opportunities to give generously to people in need. This tradition finds its origin in the Mosaic covenant in the Old Testament, where God's people were instructed to care for the poor (Deuteronomy 15:7–11). It was carried through to the New Testament church, where Paul organized a collection for believers in poverty in Jerusalem (1 Corinthians 16:1–4). Early church fathers like Justin Martyr, Cyprian, and Ambrose used the term *almsgiving* to encourage compassion and generosity for the poor and to overcome impulses toward greed. Generosity can become an important step for our growth as we recognize that everything we enjoy is a gift from God that we can share freely with others.

Notes

4 POWER IN HUMILITY

Service

Power in Humility

Chickens have a bad reputation for it, but they aren't the only creatures who regulate society by a pecking order. In a yard full of chickens, the largest and strongest chickens will demonstrate their elevated position by parading around and fluffing out their feathers. If any other chicken challenges their dominance, they will resort to pecking—brutal attacks with sharp, pointed beaks.

People often do the same type of thing—just without beaks and feathers. Even if our goal is not quite to be the first, it's definitely to avoid being the last.

Avoiding last place preoccupied the disciples' attention as they awkwardly waited for supper to begin. No one wanted to step forward and take the role of a servant by washing the feet of their peers. But then their Master did something that no one expected. Jesus showed what true greatness looks like. He demonstrated his authority and power by taking a position of weakness and humility. He wrapped a towel around his waist, took a basin, and washed and dried each of his disciples' feet.

Read It

Key Bible Passage

For this session, read the story of Jesus washing his disciples' feet in John 13:1–17.

Optional Reading

Read Luke's account of the Last Supper in Luke 22:1–30.

"I have set you an example that you should do as I have done for you."

JOHN 13:15

Know It

1. What are at least three statements about Jesus in John 13:1–3 that provide insight into the reason he chose to wash his disciples' feet?

- ____
- ____
- ____

2. What do Peter's responses to Jesus in verses 6–9 reveal about Peter's character and attitude?

3. What spiritual truth do you think Jesus is trying to communicate in verse 10?

Explore It

In a large upper room in Jerusalem, Jesus and his twelve disciples shared a Passover meal—a last supper before Jesus' arrest and trials. As a servant, he washed their feet before the meal. As a teacher, he explained spiritual truths. As a friend, he broke bread with them.

A Seder includes a beautiful Passover meal in the Jewish tradition that celebrates God's victory in bringing the nation of Israel out of bondage in Egypt. It anticipates the completion of all the promises God made to his people Israel. (You can read the story of the first Passover in Exodus 12:1–42.)

The form and structure for the modern Seder was not established until after the time of Jesus. But from the New Testament accounts of the Last Supper, it's clear that a great deal of continuity exists between the way Jesus celebrated Passover and the way contemporary Jews continue to observe Passover. Jesus reimagined the significance of Passover and filled it with new meaning, connecting it to the promises of the new covenant.

Seder Plate with Matzah

PASSOVER AND SEDER	JESUS' SACRIFICE
In the middle of the Seder, a piece of matzah (bread) is broken and eaten. The matzah is flat, scorched from the oven with what appears to be stripes, and is pierced with many holes.	Jesus' body was beaten and striped from the cords of a whip, pierced with nails and a spear, and broken for us. "He took bread, gave thanks and broke it, and gave it to them, saying, 'This is my body given for you; do this in remembrance of me'" (Luke 22:19).
Before and after the Seder meal, cups of wine are drunk to symbolize God's redemption and rescue of his people.	"After the supper he took the cup, saying, 'This cup is the new covenant in my blood, which is poured out for you'" (Luke 22:20).
At the first Passover (recorded in Exodus 12), a lamb was slaughtered and its blood applied to each house for protection against the death of their firstborn children. Then it was roasted and eaten. However, not a bone of that lamb was to be broken.	"The soldiers therefore came and broke the legs of the first man who had been crucified with Jesus, and then those of the other. But when they came to Jesus and found that he was already dead, they did not break his legs" (John 19:32–33).
In the first Passover, God brought freedom to his chosen people, Israel, while in slavery in Egypt.	Jesus brought freedom to all who trust in him through his sacrificial death and resurrection. He laid down his life to seal God's new covenant with us.

Live It

At the beginning of a Passover meal, the host dips his hands into water for ceremonial washing. Jesus took this practice to the furthest degree and began his meal by washing his disciples' feet.

One ancient Jewish text reveals that rabbis in the second century AD considered washing feet to be so menial that a Hebrew slave should not perform that act, although a son or a student could show devotion and care by willingly washing the feet of their father or teacher.

> A Hebrew slave must not wash the feet of his master, nor put his shoes on him, nor carry his things before when going to the bathhouse . . . over your brothers the children of Israel you shall not rule, one over another, with rigor. . . . But one's son or pupil may do so. (*Mekilta de Rabbi Ishmael*)

In John 13:15, Jesus points out that he is calling his disciples to follow his example. In the Greek text, the word *example* (*hypodeigma*) is actually the first word in the sentence, indicating that it is the point of emphasis. This word means "pattern." Jesus is saying, *I have formed a living blueprint, and I want your life to be a living representation of the model I have just given you.*

Life Application Questions

1. Look again at verses 1, 2, and 11 in John 13, and consider Jesus' act of humility and service in this context. What does this reveal about our Lord and his love?

2. Think of someone you know who lives their life with a servant's heart. What traits do you notice in their character and their actions?

3. Recall a time when someone completed a significant act of service for you. How did you feel and respond? What did your response indicate about your attitude or how you view service?

4. How is Jesus' example of leadership and exercise of authority different from or similar to your experiences of leadership and authority?

5. Pay attention to the double meaning in this phrase in John 13:1: "loved them to the end." Jesus loved until the end of his life, but he also loved to the most extreme point or to the uttermost degree. Remember that you are loved. How has all of humanity experienced or seen the love of Jesus? How have you personally experienced and been shaped by his love?

6. What would it mean for you to take up Jesus' challenge to follow his example and "wash" another's feet? Identify three ways you could follow his example this week.

Spiritual Discipline: Service

Don't choose to serve, *become* a servant. When we choose to serve, we can also choose to stop serving. *Becoming* a servant means that we are available and vulnerable. We put ourselves in a position of weakness, just like Jesus did when he knelt in front of his disciples to wash their feet. Here are a few suggestions that might help you become a servant.

- **Listen.** Our world can become very lonely. Giving your time and active attention to the concerns and needs of another can be an act of true service and offer you a different perspective on your own needs.
- **Be hospitable.** Hospitality is about welcoming others into the space God has given you. You may be able to host special meals, gatherings, or study groups. You might be able to create a guest room in your home for traveling friends to use. You could welcome visitors into your church and invite them to lunch. You could do something special for a new person at work to make him or her feel welcome. Bottom line, it's about allowing what God has given you to become available for others.
- **Encourage.** This word means to put courage into another. No human being alive is beyond the need to hear words affirming their value and inspiring them to never give up and to keep moving forward.
- **Surprise someone.** Simple, unexpected actions that demonstrate concern and kindness can be life-giving for you and for the person you are serving. Consider how you can reach out in unexpected ways to let someone else know that they aren't alone or that you care for them.
- **Receive service.** This can be one of the most challenging aspects of service. It's what stumped Peter when Jesus wanted to wash his feet. Being unable to allow someone

else to reach out to serve you is a sign of pride and self-reliance, not humility. When we allow someone to serve us, we acknowledge their position, value, and authority in God's kingdom and create a pathway for their growth, as well as our own.

Prayer

Lord Jesus, thank you for becoming the servant who has made new life possible for me. Help me to stop being preoccupied with my own status and agenda, and instead serve others without any strings attached. Please work through my life to demonstrate your love to those around me who need it most. Amen.

"Being the servant of all, I am bound to serve all and to administer the balm-bearing words of my Lord."

—FRANCIS OF ASSISI

Notes

Notes

5 VICTORIOUS FAILURE

Contemplation

Victorious Failure

Irony is a communication or literary technique where what appears to be true on the surface actually reveals an opposite truth. Today, we often use irony in humor. However, in the Greek tradition, irony was most often used in dramatic, tragic plays.

The scene described in Mark 15 appears on the surface to be a tragic failure and an end to life. Jesus is standing before his accusers and offering no defense. Jesus is sentenced to death, flogged, and nailed to a cross where he gives up his last breath.

But, ironically, there is a hidden victory that forms the backdrop to this tragic scene. In reality, it is the beginning of an entirely new way of living. The cross of Jesus becomes the victory of God's love over all.

Read It

Key Bible Passage

For this session, read the crucifixion story in Mark 15:1–39.

Optional Reading

Each gospel author provides different details of the same event from their unique perspective. Read all of their accounts of the crucifixion (it takes only twenty minutes or so) in Matthew 26–27, Luke 22–23, and John 18–19.

> "When the centurion, who stood there in front of Jesus, saw how he died, he said, 'Surely this man was the Son of God!'"
>
> MARK 15:39

Know It

1. How is Jesus contrasted with Barabbas in this passage? What can we learn from that contrast? How is our forgiveness and freedom in Jesus foreshadowed by Barabbas's unexpected release from prison?

2. Notice how Jesus is consistently connected to the title "King of the Jews" (Mark 15:2, 9, 12, 18, 26, 32). This title forms the basis for mockery from Jews and gentiles alike. Why is this so strongly emphasized?

3. How did different characters in this passage respond to Jesus? Jot down what you observe about their words and actions toward Jesus.

- The Sanhedrin (verse 1): ______________________________

  ____

- Pilate (verses 2–5, 15): ______________________________

  ____

- The crowd (verses 8–14): ______________________________

  ____

- Soldiers (verses 16–25): ______________________________

  ____

- Onlookers (verses 29–32): ______________________________

  ____

- Two rebels crucified (verses 27, 32): ____________________

  ____

- The centurion (verse 39): ______________________________

  ____

Explore It

Mark tailored his gospel for a Roman audience and included significant details, easy for us to miss, that would have been clear to his original audience. When Roman armies won a great victory and returned to Rome, they would take part in a triumphal march. Victorious generals would lead a procession through the streets of Rome in a civil and religious celebration of the might of the Roman Empire. Some generals even used these triumph marches as a springboard to claim Rome's throne and rule the empire. Every Roman triumph march was carefully planned and followed the same pattern. This pattern is also found in Mark's account of Jesus' crucifixion.

The Triumph of Titus
by Lawrence Alma-Tadema

ROMAN TRIUMPH MARCH	CRUCIFIXION OF JESUS Mark 15:16–24
The march began at the Praetorium.	"The soldiers led Jesus away into the palace (that is, the Praetorium)
The whole cohort was called together and formed up.	and called together the whole company of soldiers.
The general was clothed in purple, a royal color illegal for those of lower ranks to wear.	They put a purple robe on him,
The general received a victor's crown.	then twisted together a crown of thorns and set it on him.
Soldiers announced their allegiance, while placards or signs were carried proclaiming the general's victory.	And they began to call out to him, 'Hail, king of the Jews!' Again and again they struck him on the head with a staff and spit on him. Falling on their knees, they paid homage to him. . . .
An official in the parade would carry a double-bladed ax, followed by a sacrificial bull.	Then they led him out to crucify him. A certain man from Cyrene, Simon. . . was passing by on his way in from the country, and they forced him to carry the cross.
They marched through the streets until reaching the Capitoline Hill, or literally, "the place of the head," at the temple of Jupiter.	They brought Jesus to the place called Golgotha (which means 'the place of the skull').
The general was offered wine to drink, but he would refuse and pour it onto the altar or the bull.	Then they offered him wine mixed with myrrh, but he did not take it.
The bull was then sacrificed.	And they crucified him."

The Temple Veils

The temple in Jerusalem was seen as the gateway between heaven and earth in the Jewish mind-set. It was the place that represented God's presence in this world.

Mark 15:37–38 states, "Jesus breathed his last. The curtain of the temple was torn [*schizo*] in two from top to bottom." There were actually two temple veils (or curtains): the outer veil that separated the outer court from the outside world, and the inner veil that separated the innermost sanctum of the temple (the Holy of Holies) from the outer courtyards. Based on Paul's commentary about the tearing of the veil (see Ephesians 2:11–22), it seems that at least the outer veil was torn at this moment, if not both veils.

This was no flimsy curtain or delicate bride's veil. The outer veil was as thick as a man's hand, up to seventy-five feet high and at least thirty feet wide. It was a massive, woven curtain, beautifully decorated. Depictions of the basic elements of life—fire, earth, air, and water—covered the veil.

Mark uses the verb *schizo* one other time. In Mark 1:10, the heavens were "torn open" (*schizo*) for the Spirit of God to descend upon the Son of God just after his baptism at the beginning of his public ministry. Here in Mark 15, as Jesus' life ended, the veil was ripped in two from top to bottom, as if the finger of God sliced it in half.

The veil's purpose was to separate sinful humanity from a holy God. When Jesus' body was torn, the separation between God and humanity was removed. God is unleashed into the world and is making for himself a renewed people of all those who trust in Jesus' finished work on the cross!

Live It

It is difficult to imagine a form of death more horrible and humiliating than death on a cross, preceded by a mock trial, beatings, and abuse that's designed to shame.

This is the type of death that Jesus endured and that divine wisdom selected. If we can come to terms with the truth that Jesus had to give his life as a substitute for us, we are still faced with the question of why it had to be *this* death. Why not a more peaceful way? What might God have been accomplishing through choosing this most terrible method for death?

Reflect on these questions. Contemplate the suffering that Jesus endured for us. Stand at the foot of the cross at Golgotha, look upon Jesus, and declare with the centurion, "Surely this man was the Son of God!" (Mark 15:39).

> "He received the spittle of revilers, who, a short time before, with his spittle had cured the eyes of a blind man. . . . He was stripped of his earthly garment, who clothes others in the vestment of immortality. . . . He was given vinegar to drink, who offered the cup of salvation. He, the innocent and just—indeed, innocence and justice itself—is counted among transgressors, and truth concealed by false witnesses. He who is judge is judged, and the Word of God is silently led to the slaughter."
>
> —CYPRIAN, EARLY CHURCH FATHER

Life Application Questions

1. Consider how people in the time of Jesus responded to the crucifixion of Jesus. How are people still responding to his cross today? How have you responded?

2. Read Romans 3:23–25, 2 Corinthians 5:21, and Colossians 1:21–22. According to these Bible passages, what did Jesus' sacrifice on the cross accomplish for us?

3. Before his crucifixion, Jesus called his followers to "take up your cross" (Matthew 16:24; Mark 8:34; Luke 9:23). What does it mean for you to follow Jesus in the way of the cross?

4. Christianity is the only faith that holds at its core the humility of its God. How does Jesus' suffering and identification with humiliation and weakness change your perspective about life and suffering?

5. How was God turning suffering into victory with the cross of Jesus? How has he done that in your past?

6. What are you facing now that you would like to give over to God so he can turn your tragedy into triumph?

Spiritual Discipline: Contemplation

The Christian practice of contemplation (or meditation) involves becoming quiet in order to create space for Jesus to work within us, leading us closer to himself so we can keep following after him. Some Christians are frightened of these terms or ideas because of the practices of Eastern religions, like Buddhism. Meditation in Eastern religions strives for detachment from the world and emptying the mind. Christian contemplation moves us toward attachment to Jesus and filling the mind with thoughts of God and his Word.

Here are few suggestions to begin this practice:

1. **Set aside a time.** Create space in your schedule to devote uninterrupted attention to God himself, who he is, and what he has done.
2. **Set aside a place.** Find a quiet space, perhaps outdoors or maybe sitting on a porch or deck, and remove possible distractions like phones.
3. **Select a Bible passage, word, or idea.** You may find that one verse, phrase, or section from this current study has attracted your mind. Allow yourself to internalize and personalize that message and allow it to sink down into your soul.

Meditating on God and his Word creates space for him to remodel your interior life. Don't be discouraged if you get distracted or find it awkward at first. Your efforts will be rewarded in time.

Prayer

Jesus, you are the only innocent one and you took on the sins of the world and suffered a death that you did not deserve. You were despised and rejected and mocked. You exposed our false visions of justice. In your march to Golgotha, Calvary's hill, you claimed the victor's crown.

Don't allow us to be shocked at those who still respond to you with open hostility. Don't let us slip into the camp of those who treat you politely, but fail to grasp the claim you have placed over our entire life. Help us to continue standing amazed at the sight of your cross and your crown, exclaiming with the centurion, *You are the Son of God!* Amen.

Notes

Notes

Celebration

Living Hope

The Milky Way Galaxy—home to earth, the sun, and countless other stars and planets—revolves around a powerful gravitational center. The movements of everything in our galaxy take shape around what astrophysicists believe to be a black hole. Black holes exert immense gravitational force because they are the remains of massive stars that have burned out and have imploded, collapsing on themselves. The existence of black holes is difficult to prove because they are essentially invisible. But on April 10, 2019, the first images of light warping around a black hole were released, providing the first visual evidence of a black hole.

Jesus came into this world as light penetrating darkness. He was and is true God of true God and light from light. His life was a demonstration of the power and glory of God, and also of the immeasurable grace and acceptance that God offers us. On the cross, his light—his love—burned brightly. Then, his light was extinguished and hidden inside a darkened tomb. On the third day after his death, Jesus took up his life again in resurrection and left the tomb behind.

All of life, human history, and our own faith revolves around the darkness of Jesus' empty tomb.

Read It

Key Bible Passage

For this session, read the story of the resurrection in Luke 24:1–49.

Optional Reading

Read the parallel accounts of the resurrection in Matthew 28:1–20, Mark 16:1–8, and John 20:1–29.

Observe the similarities and differences between the unique perspectives of each gospel writer.

> "Why do you look for the living among the dead? He is not here; he has risen!"
>
> LUKE 24:5–6

Know It

1. What do you suppose the followers of Jesus felt and thought just after their Lord was crucified? How about after they saw the empty tomb? And then after he appeared to them? Is there any indication that they expected Jesus to rise from the dead?

2. What can you learn about Jesus' resurrection body from Luke 24?

Verses 15–16: ______________________________

____

Verses 30–31: ______________________________

____

Verses 36–37: ______________________________

____

Verses 38–40: ______________________________________

____

Verses 41–43: ______________________________________

____

How might this inform your expectations or hopes about the future resurrection bodies that believers in Jesus will enjoy?

3. What do you observe in the story of the resurrection that encourages your faith and confidence that Jesus defeated death and offers new life to us?

Explore It

At the heart of our Christian faith is the firmly held belief that Jesus rose from the dead. This belief is also a stumbling block for those who don't believe in an afterlife and who deny that miracles like this could occur.

Our faith is not dependent on reason; however, our faith in the resurrection is reasonable. Here are some reasons why:

1. Jesus certainly lived and died.

The gospel writers provide significant details from their experience of Jesus' death, but sources outside of Christianity from the first and second centuries were also aware of Jesus, his life, his death, and his reported resurrection. The Roman historian Tacitus wrote about Emperor Nero blaming Christians for burning Rome:

Gaius Cornelius Tacitus

> Nero set up as the culprits and punished with the utmost refinement of cruelty a class hated for their abominations, who are commonly called Christians. Christus, from whom their name is derived, was executed at the hands of the procurator Pontius Pilate in the reign of Tiberius. Checked for the moment, this pernicious superstition again broke out, not only in Judea, the source of evil, but even in Rome.
> (*Annales, xv. 44, The Neronian Persecution*, c. AD 64)

2. The disciples were radically changed.

The portrait of the disciples that emerges just after Jesus' death describes a group of skeptical, fearful, hopeless men (see Matthew 28:17; Luke 24:21; John 20:19). Yet, after repeatedly interacting with Jesus following his resurrection, this same group of Jewish peasants from an ignored corner of the Roman Empire became dynamic, courageous witnesses of the resurrection. They began a movement that would lead most of them to a martyr's death, but would also subvert world powers, change the world, and alter the course of history (see Acts 2:24; 3:15; 4:2).

3. The tomb was empty.

No one ever produced the corpse of Jesus. This would have been the simplest and fastest way to debunk stories about his resurrection. If the Roman government or the Jewish leaders possessed or could obtain his body or bones, they could have quickly put an end to the fast-spreading word that Jesus had risen from the dead. They didn't. The best they could do was begin a rumor that Jesus' disciples had stolen his body.

4. World history was altered.

In the several centuries before and after Jesus' life, multiple individuals raised up rebellions to try to obtain Jewish independence and claim the fulfillment of God's promises to his people. Every one of these so-called messiah figures ended in the same way—a horrible death.

About thirty years after Jesus' death and resurrection, a man named Simon ben Giora helped incite a Jewish revolt with limited success against the Romans, even pushing Roman forces out of parts of Judea. Rome responded with great force and devastated the entire region. They led a triumphal march with thousands of captives back to Rome, where Simon was executed.

None of these messiah figures maintained a following after their death, because they clearly died and remained dead. But, not only did the movement around Jesus continue after his death, it dramatically grew. The only possible explanation is that God did something unexpected that had never happened before by resurrecting Jesus from the dead.

5. The details in the gospels demonstrate the truth of the claims.

If the gospel writers were merely concocting a story about how Jesus had risen from the dead, they could have created a more believable lie. Instead, they recorded simple, straightforward accounts of the events surrounding the resurrection.

The first witnesses to the resurrection and messengers of the good news about Jesus were invalid according to Jewish law. In the Mishnah, the legal code for the practice of the Jewish law by rabbis, women were not considered reliable or admissible witnesses: "This is the governing principle: Any evidence which a woman is not valid to offer, also they are not valid to offer" (*Ros Hassannah 1.8*).

Mary Magdalene and the Holy Women at the Tomb by James Tissot

According to the gospels, the first witnesses of the empty tomb were women: "Very early in the morning, the women took the spices they had prepared and went to the tomb. . . . They did not find the body of the Lord Jesus. . . . It was Mary Magdalene, Joanna, Mary the mother of James, and the others with them" (Luke 24:1–3, 10). If the resurrection was just a made-up story, the gospel writers would've made up witnesses who were men of standing, instead of women who were barred from testifying. This suggests that the gospel writers were simply telling the story as it really occurred.

Jesus' followers did not anticipate the resurrection or initially believe it, even when confronted with evidence. Had they stolen Jesus' body or participated in a deception, they would have likely cast themselves in a better light. Instead, the gospels record that "the story sounded like nonsense to the men, so they didn't believe it" (Luke 24:11). Even after seeing Jesus, not all of the disciples were immediately convinced it could be true: "When they saw him, they worshiped him; but some doubted" (Matthew 28:17).

Some details of the resurrection story create obstacles to belief, yet the original witnesses included these details. They would not have done so if they wanted to convince people of a lie, but only if they were committed to reporting the truth of their experience. For example, not everyone recognized Jesus immediately. The disciples on the road to Emmaus and Mary outside the tomb both initially mistook Jesus for someone else (Luke 24:13–16; John 20:11, 14).

Live It

A group of four-year-olds were gathered in a Sunday school class in Chattanooga. The teacher, looking at her class, asked enthusiastically, "Does anyone know what today is?" One little girl knew. "It's Palm Sunday!" she said. "Very good," said the teacher. "And does anyone know what next Sunday is?" The same little girl lifted her hand again. "Yes, next Sunday is Easter," she announced. The teacher was very pleased with this little girl, and she complimented her effusively before asking a third question. "Now, does anyone know what makes Easter so special?" It was the same little girl who again raised her hand and offered this answer: "Yes, next Sunday is Easter because Jesus rose from the dead." Before the teacher could compliment her, she kept on talking: "But if he sees his shadow, he has to go back in for seven weeks."

(From *Preacher's Sourcebook of Creative Sermon Illustrations*, Robert Morgan; Thomas Nelson, 2007; 254.)

While most of us certainly know the difference between Easter and Groundhog Day, we might not fully understand the meaning of Easter, just like that little girl. Maybe we get caught up in an emotional Easter celebration, or we're just keeping up with a tradition. Either way, we fail to grasp how the reality of Jesus' victory over death opens up a pathway to new life for us and to renewal for all of God's world.

Easter Celebration

Many of us may enjoy a sunrise Easter celebration, where we sit in the cool darkness waiting for the light of the sun to bring warmth and the promise of new life. Sunrise services find their roots in the Easter Vigil of the early church, dating as far back as the second century. The vigil takes place at night between sunset and sunrise, as the first celebration of the resurrection.

The different parts of the service depend on the traditions of a particular church, but they often include the following:

Ceremonies Involving Light: In some churches, the sanctuary is kept dark like a tomb with the choir waiting inside. Worshipers gather outside and light candles. The doors to the church are flung open and light fills the darkened space as praise to God for bringing new life. An old European tradition included villagers returning home from the Easter Vigil to light their fireplaces with their candles. This was a symbol of the light received and the light believers are for Jesus.

Baptism: Those who have been preparing to join with the church and publicly express their faith through baptism often take this important step during the Easter Vigil. In the early church, the forty days before Easter was the time when newcomers learned the Christian faith and formally entered the church.

Special Readings: Various passages from the Old Testament and the Gospels are read to explain the significance of Easter. Often these readings focus on the night of creation when darkness turned to light; the night when Abraham offered his son Isaac until a ram became a substitute sacrifice; the night of Passover when God rescued the nation of Israel from slavery in Egypt; and the night of Jesus' burial before he rose to new life.

Communion: Jesus' broken body and poured out blood are remembered and shared. His sacrifice is our source of strength, forgiveness, and new life.

Singing: An old song that is often sung during the vigil proclaims, "Rejoice heavenly powers! Sing, choirs of angels! Exult, all creation around God's throne! Jesus Christ, our King, is risen!"

Life Application Questions

1. How does Jesus' resurrection give us hope for the future, including life after death and God's plan for the world? How does it give us hope for the present, in both the mundane and the exceptional circumstances of life?

2. Have you ever struggled to believe the truth of the resurrection or questioned the accuracy of the gospel story? What helped your faith grow?

3. How could you be part of helping other people believe and be changed by the hope and power of Jesus' resurrection? Consider writing down three specific ways that the living hope that you enjoy could spread or be shared with others.

4. Read Philippians 3:10 about Paul's ultimate aim in life. How does Paul describe what it means "to know Christ"? What does life look like when we join in Jesus' suffering and also in the power of the resurrection?

5. Reflect back on this journey to the resurrection. Over these six sessions, where has God been taking you? What have you learned? How are you changing?

6. What work of new life do you hope God will do in and through you? Write a prayer to the Lord, asking him in specific ways to bring the living hope of Jesus' resurrection into practical operation in your life now.

Spiritual Discipline: Celebration

Joy gives us strength and helps us fully experience the best parts of life and survive the harshest challenges. We often move toward imitations of joy or attempts to manufacture joy by amusing ourselves with distractions. But true joy most often rises up out of a life of faithfulness to God. Sometimes we are so busy with the daily stresses and details of life that we forget to pause and create space for heartfelt celebration.

Easter is a season when we remember God smiling on us by bringing new life out of death. It's a cause for great celebration!

Here are a few suggestions for celebration:

- **Make some noise.** Singing, laughter, funny stories, praising God—all of these are expressions of the life God has given us. It's difficult to celebrate and remain silent.
- **Be creative.** Making moments of celebration is possible through both careful planning and awareness of God's presence with us in every moment of life. One of my fondest parenting memories is pausing after planting flowers in the spring with my children to close our eyes, remember the cold barren wintertime, and then open our eyes to the beauty and new life of spring all around us and thank God for always bringing us new life.
- **Connect with others.** Celebrations happen best with other people. If you are doing this Bible study in a group, then plan a special meal, barbecue, or other gathering to have fun together and celebrate what God is doing in your lives. Take advantage of special holidays, like Easter, to gather with family or friends and share the joy of living in God's light together.

Prayer

Lord, we want to know you. We want to know the power of your resurrection, and we understand that means we will also join the fellowship of your suffering. Help us to be living representations of who you are. Help us to do justice and love mercy, to heal relationships, to confront lovingly, to resist temptation, to find and hold on to true freedom. Help us to be part of bringing the living hope of Easter and resurrection into our present realities. Amen.

"With Easter, God's new creation is launched upon a surprised world, pointing ahead to the renewal, the redemption, the rebirth of the entire creation . . . every act of love, every deed done in Christ and by the Spirit, every work of true creativity—doing justice, making peace, healing families, resisting temptation, seeking and winning true freedom—is an earthly event in a long history of things that implement Jesus's own resurrection and anticipate the final new creation and act as signposts of hope, pointing back to the first and on to the second."

—N. T. Wright

Notes

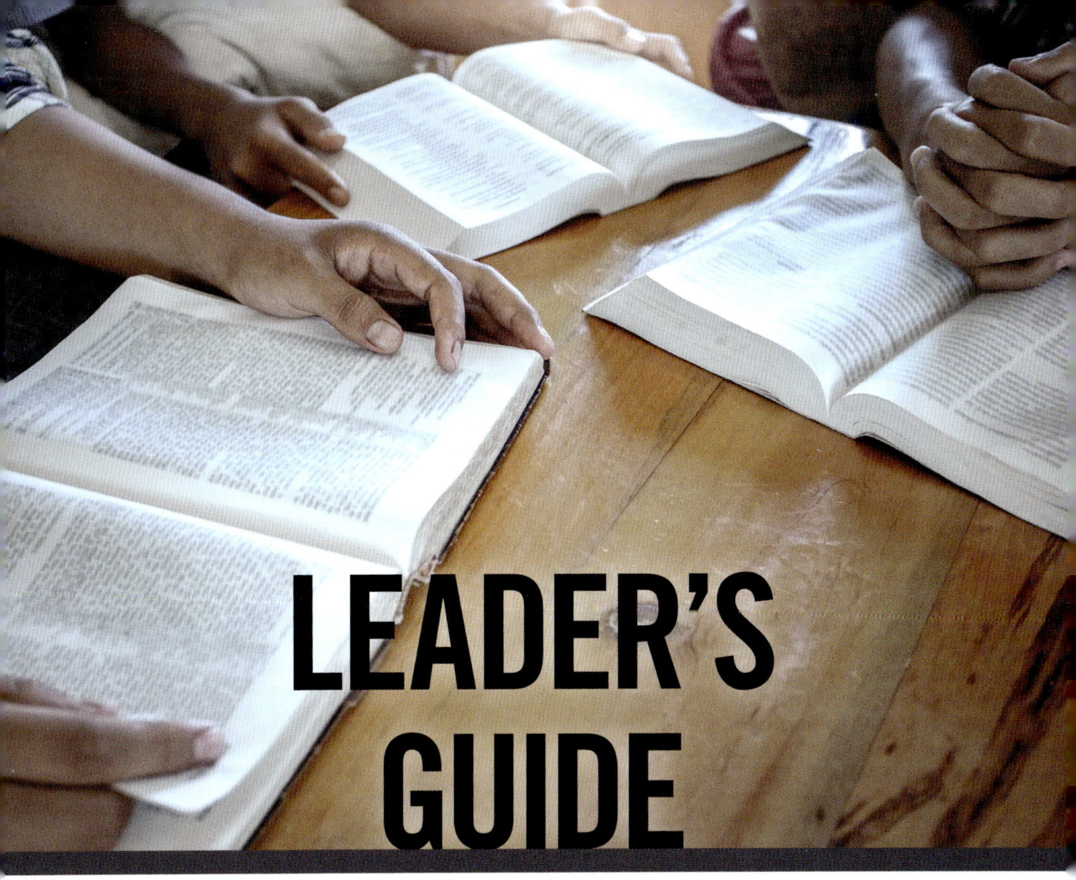

LEADER'S GUIDE

"Encourage one another and build each other up."

1 THESSALONIANS 5:11

Leader's Guide

Congratulations! You've either decided to lead a Bible study, or you're thinking hard about it. Guess what? God does big things through small groups. When his people gather together, open his Word, and invite his Spirit to work, their lives are changed!

Do you feel intimidated yet?

Be comforted by this: even the great apostle Paul felt "in over his head" at times. When he went to Corinth to help people grasp God's truth, he admitted he was overwhelmed: "I came to you in weakness with great fear and trembling" (1 Corinthians 2:3). Later he wondered, "Who is adequate for such a task as this?" (2 Corinthians 2:16 NLT).

Feelings of inadequacy are normal; every leader has them. What's more, they're actually healthy. They keep us dependent on the Lord. It is in our times of greatest weakness that God works most powerfully. The Lord assured Paul, "My grace is sufficient for you, for my power is made perfect in weakness" (2 Corinthians 12:9).

The Goal

What is the goal of a Bible study group? Listen as the apostle Paul speaks to Christians:

- "Oh, my dear children! I feel as if I'm going through labor pains for you again, and they will continue until *Christ is fully developed in your lives*" (Galatians 4:19 NLT, emphasis added).
- "For God knew his people in advance, and he chose them *to become like his Son*" (Romans 8:29 NLT, emphasis added).

Do you see it? God's ultimate goal for us is that we would become like Jesus Christ. This means a Bible study is not about filling our heads with more information. Rather, it is about undergoing transformation. We study and apply God's truth so that it will reshape our hearts and minds, and so that, over time we will become more and more like Jesus.

Paul said, "The purpose of my instruction is that all believers would be filled with love that comes from a pure heart, a clear conscience, and genuine faith" (1 Timothy 1:5 NLT).

This isn't about trying to "master the Bible." No, we're praying that God's Word will master us, and through humble submission to its authority, we'll be changed from the inside out.

Your Role

Many group leaders experience frustration because they confuse their role with God's role. Here's the truth: God alone knows our deep hang-ups and hurts. Only he can save a soul, heal a heart, fix a life. It is God who rescues people from depression, addictions, bitterness, guilt, and shame. We Bible study leaders need to realize that *we can't do any of those things.*

So what can we do? More than we think!

- We can pray.
- We can trust God to work powerfully.
- We can obey the Spirit's promptings.
- We can prepare for group gatherings.
- We can keep showing up faithfully.

With group members:

- We can invite, remind, encourage, and love.
- We can ask good questions and then listen attentively.
- We can gently speak tough truths.
- We can celebrate with those who are happy and weep with those who are sad.
- We can call and text and let them know we've got their back.

But we can never do the things that only the Almighty can do.

- We can't play the Holy Spirit in another person's life.
- We can't be in charge of outcomes.
- We can't force God to work according to our timetables.

And one more important reminder: besides God's role and our role, group members also have a key role to play in this process. If they don't show up, prepare, or open their hearts to God's transforming truth, no life change will take place. We're not called to manipulate or shame, pressure or arm twist. We're not to blame if members don't make progress—and we don't get the credit when they do. We're mere instruments in the hands of God.

"I planted the seed, [another] watered it, but God has been making it grow. So neither the one who plants nor the one who waters is anything, but only God, who makes things grow."

1 CORINTHIANS 3:6–7

Leader Myths and Truths

Many people assume that a Bible study leader should:

- Be a Bible scholar.
- Be a dynamic communicator.
- Have a big, fancy house to meet in.
- Have it all together—no doubts, bad habits, or struggles.

These are myths—even outright lies of the enemy!

Here's the truth:

- God is looking for humble Bible students, not scholars.
- You're not signing up to give lectures, you're agreeing to facilitate discussions.
- You don't need a palace, just a place where you can have uninterrupted discussions. (Perhaps one of your group members will agree to host your study.)
- Nobody has it all together. We are all in process. We are all seeking to work out "our salvation with fear and trembling" (Philippians 2:12).

As long as your desire is that Jesus be Lord of your life, God will use you!

Some Bad Reasons to Lead a Group

- You want to wow others with your biblical knowledge.

  "Love . . . does not boast, it is not proud" (1 Corinthians 13:4).

- You're seeking a hidden personal gain or profit.

  "We do not peddle the word of God for profit" (2 Corinthians 2:17).

- You want to tell people how wrong they are.

  "Do not condemn" (Romans 2:1).

- You want to fix or rescue people.

  "It is God who works in you to will and to act" (Philippians 2:13).

- You're being pressured to do it.

  "Am I now trying to win the approval of human beings, or of God?" (Galatians 1:10).

A Few Do's

✔ Pray for your group.

Are you praying for your group members regularly? It is the most important thing a leader can do for his or her group.

✔ Ask for help.

If you're new at leading, spend time with an experienced group leader and pick his or her brain.

✔ Encourage members to prepare.

Challenge participants to read the Bible passages and the material in their study guides, and to answer and reflect on the study questions during the week prior to meeting.

✔ Discuss the group guidelines.

Go over important guidelines with your group at the first session, and again as needed if new members join the group in later sessions. See the *Group Guidelines* at the end of this leader's guide.

✔ Share the load.

Don't be a one-person show. Ask for volunteers. Let group members host the meeting, arrange for snacks, plan socials, lead group prayer times, and so forth. The old saying is true: Participants become boosters; spectators become critics.

✔ Be flexible.

If a group member shows up in crisis, it is okay to stop and take time to surround the hurting brother or sister with love. Provide a safe place for sharing. Listen and pray for his or her needs.

✔ Be kind.

Remember, there's a story—often a heart-breaking one—behind every face. This doesn't *excuse* bad or disruptive behavior on the part of group members, but it might *explain* it.

A Few Don'ts

✘ Don't "wing it."

Although these sessions are designed to require minimum preparation, read each one ahead of time. Highlight the questions you feel are especially important for your group to spend time on.

✘ Don't feel ashamed to say, "I don't know."

Disciple means "learner," not "know-it-all."

✘ Don't feel the need to "dump the truck."

You don't have to say everything you know. There is always next week. A little silence during group discussion time, that's fine. Let members wrestle with questions.

✘ Don't put members on the spot.

Invite others to share and pray, but don't pressure them. Give everyone an opportunity to participate. People will open up on their own time as they learn to trust the group.

✘ Don't go down "rabbit trails."

Be careful not to let one person dominate the time or for the discussion to go down the gossip road. At the same time, don't short-circuit those occasions when the Holy Spirit is working in your group members' lives and therefore they *need* to share a lot.

✘ Don't feel pressure to cover every question.

Better to have a robust discussion of four questions than a superficial conversation of ten.

✘ Don't go long.

Encourage good discussion, but don't be afraid to "rope 'em back in" when needed. Start and end on time. If you do this from the beginning, you'll avoid the tendency of group members to arrive later and later as the season goes on.

How to Use This Study Guide

Many group members have busy lives—dealing with long work hours, childcare, and a host of other obligations. These sessions are designed to be as simple and straightforward as possible to fit into a busy schedule. Nevertheless, encourage group members to set aside some time during the week (even if it's only a little) to pray, read the key Bible passage, and respond to questions in this study guide. This will make the group discussion and experience much more rewarding for everyone.

Each session contains four parts.

Read It

The *Key Bible Passage* is the portion of Scripture everyone should read during the week before the group meeting. The group can read it together at the beginning of the session as well.

The *Optional Reading* is for those who want to dig deeper and read lengthier Bible passages on their own during the week.

Know It

This section encourages participants to reflect on the Bible passage they've just read. Here, the goal is to interact with the biblical text and grasp what it says. (We'll get into practical application later.)

Explore It

Here group members can find background information with charts and visuals to help them understand the Bible passage and the topic more deeply. They'll move beyond the text itself and see how it connects to other parts of Scripture and the historical and cultural context.

Live It

Finally, participants will examine how God's Word connects to their lives. There are application questions for group discussion or personal reflection, practical ideas to apply what they've learned from God's Word, and a closing thought and/or prayer. (Remember, you don't have to cover all the questions or everything in this section during group time. Focus on what's most important for your group.)

Celebrate!

Here's an idea: Have a plan for celebrating your time together after the last session of this Bible study. Do something special after your gathering time, or plan a separate celebration for another time and place. Maybe someone in your group has the gift of hospitality—let them use their gifting and organize the celebration.

	30-MINUTE SESSION	60-MINUTE SESSION
READ IT	Open in prayer and read the *Key Bible Passage.* 5 minutes	Open in prayer and read the *Key Bible Passage.* 5 minutes
KNOW IT	Ask: "What stood out to you from this Bible passage?" 5 minutes	Ask: "What stood out to you from this Bible passage?" 5 minutes
EXPLORE IT	Encourage group members to read this section on their own, but don't spend group time on it. Move on to the life application questions.	Ask: "What did you find new or helpful in the *Explore It* section? What do you still have questions about?" 10 minutes
LIVE IT	Members voluntarily share their answers to 3 or 4 of the life application questions. 15 minutes	Members voluntarily share their answers to the life application questions. 25 minutes
PRAYER & CLOSING	Conclude with a brief prayer. 5 minutes	Share prayer requests and praise reports. Encourage the group to pray for each other in the coming week. Conclude with a brief prayer. 15 minutes

	90-MINUTE SESSION
	Open in prayer and read the *Key Bible Passage.* 5 minutes
	• Ask: "What stood out to you from this Bible passage?" • Then go over the *Know It* questions as a group. 10 minutes
	• Ask: "What did you find new or helpful in the *Explore It* section? What do you still have questions about?" • Here, the leader can add information found while preparing for the session. • If there are questions or a worksheet in this section, go over those as a group. 20 minutes
	• Members voluntarily share their answers to the life application questions. • Wrap up this time with a closing thought or suggestions for how to put into practice in the coming week what was just learned from God's Word. 30 minutes
	• Share prayer requests and praise reports. • Members voluntarily pray during group time about the requests and praises shared. • Encourage the group to pray for each other in the coming week. 25 minutes

Group Guidelines

This group is about discovering God's truth, supporting each other, and finding growth in our new life in Christ. To reach these goals, a group needs a few simple guidelines that everyone should follow for the group to stay healthy and for trust to develop.

1. **Everyone agrees to make group time a priority.**
   We understand that there are work, health, and family issues that come up. So if there is an emergency or schedule conflict that cannot be avoided, be sure to let someone know that you can't make it that week. This may seem like a small thing, but it makes a big difference to your other group members.
2. **What is said in the group stays in the group.**
   Accept it now: we are going to share some personal things. Therefore, the group must be a safe and confidential place to share.
3. **Don't be judgmental, even if you strongly disagree.**
   Listen first, and contribute your perspective only as needed. Remember, you don't fully know someone else's story. Take this advice from James: "Be quick to listen, slow to speak, and slow to become angry" (James 1:19).
4. **Be patient with one another.**
   We are all in process, and some of us are hurting and struggling more than others. Don't expect bad habits or attitudes to disappear overnight.
5. **Everyone participates.**
   It may take time to learn how to share, but as you develop a trust toward the other group members, take the chance.

If you struggle in any of these areas, ask God's help for growth, and ask the group to help hold you accountable. Remember, you're all growing together.

Notes

ROSE VISUAL BIBLE STUDIES

6-Session Study Guides for Personal or Group Use

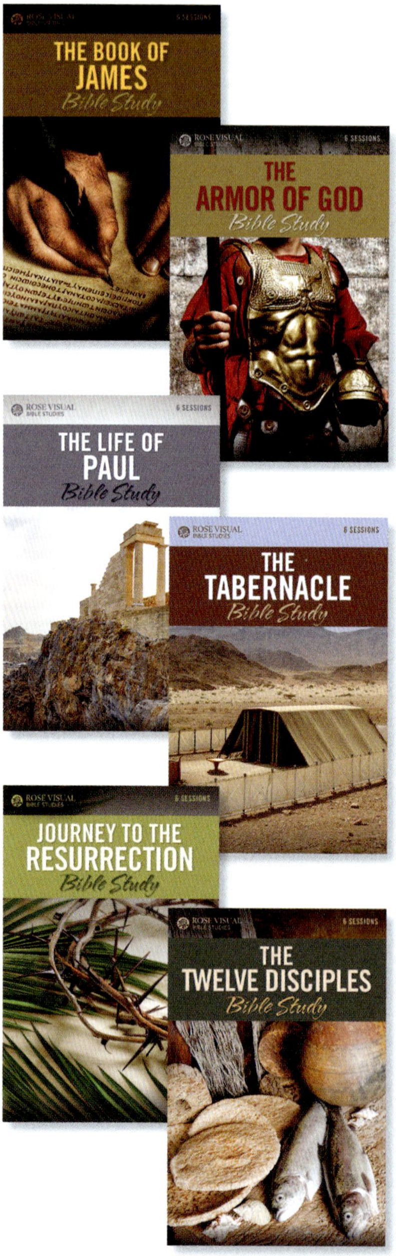

THE BOOK OF JAMES

Find out what James says about cultivating a genuine living faith through six tests of faith.

ISBN 9781628627589

THE ARMOR OF GOD

Dig deep into Ephesians 6 and learn the meaning of each piece of the armor.

ISBN 9781628627558

THE LIFE OF PAUL

See how the apostle Paul persevered through trials and proclaimed the gospel.

ISBN 9781628627619

THE TABERNACLE

Discover how each item of the tabernacle foreshadowed Jesus and what that means for us today.

ISBN 9781628627527

JOURNEY TO THE RESURRECTION

Renew your heart and mind as you engage in spiritual practices and follow Jesus. Perfect for Easter.

ISBN 9781628628081

THE TWELVE DISCIPLES

Learn about the twelve men Jesus chose to be his disciples and what this means for all disciples today.

ISBN 9781628628098

HENDRICKSON PUBLISHERS
ROSE PUBLISHING
www.hendricksonrose.com